THE ALIGNMENT PROCESS

by DEMETRA BILLY

THE ALIGNMENT PROCESS

Charleston, SC
www.PalmettoPublishing.com

The Alignment Process

Copyright © 2022 by Demetra Billy

All rights reserved.

No portion of this book may be reproduced, stored in a retrieval system, or transmitted in any form by any means—electronic, mechanical, photocopy, recording, or other—except for brief quotations in printed reviews, without prior permission of the author.

First Edition

Hardcover ISBN: 978-1-68515-279-6
Paperback ISBN: 978-1-68515-280-2
eBook ISBN: 978-1-68515-281-9

Cover and Designs: Lady "D" Graphic Designs LLC (Demetra Billy)
Photographer: WBJ Productions (Wayne Billy Jr.)
Unless otherwise indicated, Bible quotations are taken from the King James Version.

This book is dedicated first and foremost to my Lord and Savior Jesus Christ, who saved me at the young age of fifteen and gave me a new life in him; it has been well over thirty years, and I'm still growing stronger and stronger in him every day.

To my husband of fourteen years and growing, Elder Wayne Billy Sr., thank you for always believing in me and trusting God with me through this process. I love you, sweetheart. "I love you now, I loved you then, and I love you more and more; you are my very best friend." Quoted yours truly, Demetra Billy.

To my mother, Evangelist Charlotte Catchings, thank you, Mom, for always being there for me and instilling the Word of God and prayer in me as a little girl. Making us stay in church, day and night (even when we didn't want to), and allowing God to order your steps to the church home I have today—Jesus Tabernacle of Deliverance Ministries. I am eternally grateful to call you Mom, I love you beyond words, to infinity and beyond.

To my late father, Deacon William Catchings, a loving and caring dad who always knew his daughters. Thank you for all your love and support throughout my entire life. The last words you spoke to me before going home to be with our Lord were "Whatever God tells you to do, do it and do it quickly." I will forever love you.

To my five brothers, William "Conroy," Terry, Emanuel, Dennis, and Unsail, and my three sisters, Shannon, Shawnkesha, and Michelle "TeTe," words can't express the love I have for you; thank you very much. My brother-in-love Brian, and sisters-in-love Lolita, Doretta, Felecia, I love you. All of my family, friends, and associates, thank you for your love and support.

My mentors Rochelle Saulsberry, who took me under her wings teaching me to never take "no" for an answer and remember your "yes" is always out there, I love you so much, and Bishop Designate Dr. Mable E. Allen, I'm eternally grateful for all the things you've poured into my life; I love you forever.

To the best spiritual leaders I believe ever graced this planet, Apostle David and Pastor R. Elaine Billy, who have believed in me, loved me, mentored me, rebuked me, cried with me, and prayed with me through many days and nights. Words cannot express the love I have for you, so I say thank you from the bottom of my heart—my love for you both is beyond words.

Foreword

Pastor R. Elaine Billy

Congratulations to our spiritual daughter Evangelist Demetra Catchings-Billy on her first book and of many more to come. Evangelist Demetra has been a faithful, devoted, committed, and diligent servant of the Lord Jesus Christ from her youth. Like Timothy in the Bible was taught by his grandmother and mother (2 Timothy 1:5), she has been taught from her youth through her natural parents and spiritual parents. She came to Jesus Tabernacle of Deliverance Ministries at the age of fifteen. Evangelist Demetra has observed, prayed, fasted, and studied God's word assiduously to be an aligned servant, who she is today. Evangelist Demetra has worked hard and diligently with the Senior Pastor Apostle David Billy Sr. and myself, Pastor R. Elaine Billy. There were times when Evangelist Demetra was corrected, and she received it as a true daughter of God. In the scripture, Proverbs 9:8 says, "Rebuke a wise man, and he will love thee." Evangelist Demetra would make the adjustment to correct the problem to be aligned with God and her spiritual leaders in righteousness. She is a true example of living the scriptures and aligning herself with God's word.

This book will impact and bless your life because it is from a true heart through submitting and obeying God's word in demonstration. It was inspired by the Holy Spirit to help the body of Christ. It will benefit anyone who wants to follow and please God. Apostle David Billy Sr. and I thank God and are elated that Evangelist Demetra has taken the time to put in writing the things she has observed, learned, and lived during the thirty-plus years in ministry. In times like these, this book is so relevant because many people are not enduring sound doctrine. I trust God that everyone who reads this book, *The Alignment Process*, will be blessed and enhanced to fulfill their divine purpose in life through aligning to God's perfect will and plan. So be blessed through this powerfully anointed and gifted woman of God, as she shares in this book how to align ourselves with God.

*Pastor R. Elaine Billy

Introduction

In this book, you will come to learn that our spiritual life is more important than this natural life that we are living in daily. So as it is in the natural it's even more so in the spirit. When you look at the word *alignment*, What does it mean? What does it take to stay there, and What is the outcome?

Most of the time we as a people don't realize the smallest things in life are the things that are the most important, and the smallest things are required to hold it all together. Maintenance—everything in this natural life needs maintenance, our hair, clothes, shoes, vehicles, and so on, and if we don't take the time to do the maintenance on them, these things will fall out of alignment and eventually break down and fall apart. So the same maintenance principles applies to the spirit. If we do not take the time to learn and study the word of God, our creator, our spiritual life will fall apart and eventually die. It is very important that we learn how to build our life both spiritually and naturally according to the word and will of God.

Natural alignment: Arrangement in a straight line or in a correct or appropriate relative position. A position of agreement or alliance. The act of aligning parts of a machine through "oil changes, lube jobs, and wheel alignments." The act of aligning or state of being aligned, especially, the proper positioning or state of adjustment of parts (as of a mechanical or electronic device) in relation to each other (*Merriam-Webster's Dictionary*).

People alignment: When people align and agree to go in the same direction and agree as one, this happens when one person changes to be true to another person. An example of people alignment might be "Your boss told you to dress more professionally." And you came in agreement and did so. (People alignment by Matthew Ström).

Spiritual alignment: Focusing our mind, thoughts, and conduct on the ability to live according to the true Word of God. We are living life on a path ordained by God, our creator, and are reaping the benefits of our concentration on him daily. We are to align ourselves with the Word of God and listen to hear his voice and follow his directions, not our own directions. An example of this is founded in the book of Joshua 6:5, 16, and 20. Joshua was given directions by God to march around the walls of Jericho, as he followed God's direction the walls fell down flat.

Process: A series of actions or steps taken in order to achieve a particular end. The waiting period, the place of uncertainties, the place where we are being made and our character is being constructed. The place of preparation where God teaches us, builds our character, strengthens our faith, and gives us the ability to do what he has designed for us to do before the foundation of the world. Our true calling is made in the process; all we have to do is go through the process, keeping our prayer life our lifeline of communication vertically with God in prayer and our study life, horizontally by studying and applying the Word of God in our lives daily.

Table of Contents

Dedication · v

Foreword   Pastor R. Elaine Billy · vii

Introduction · ix

Chapter 1   Understanding the Alignment Process
{Keys/Steps to Alignment} · · · · · · · · · · · · · · · · · · 1

Chapter 2   The Foundation Runs Deep
{Prayer Is Not an Option} · · · · · · · · · · · · · · · · · · 13

Chapter 3   Trusting the Process
{Studying God's Word, Not an Option} · · · · · · · · · · 21

Chapter 4   The Orchestrating Process · · · · · · · · · · · · · · · · · · 27

Chapter 5   The Shifting Process · 39

Chapter 6   Bringing It Full Circle · 45

Chapter 7   The Glorious Outcome from Staying Rooted and
            Grounded··································· 49

About the Author ··································· 59

Chapter 1

Understanding the Alignment Process
{Keys/Steps to Alignment}

Before the world began, inside the mind of God the process had already begun. The mind is the beginning of all the creation. The mind is where life begins and death ends. The mind creates what is brought to visible reality. In the beginning God created the heaven and the earth. And the earth was without form, and void; and darkness was upon the face of the deep. And the Spirit of God moved upon the face of the waters. And God said, Let there be light: and there was light, Genesis 1:1–3. For we are his workmanship, created in Christ Jesus unto good works, which God hath before ordained that we should walk in them, Ephesians 2:10.

Revealing yourself is your true Identity. Knowing who you are in the inside (spiritually) is the first step in knowing who our creator is. Why? If we were created in his image and likeness, then we must become like him. In order to be like him, we must know him, the one who created us. The Bible says, "Know ye that the Lord he is God, It is he that hath made us, and not we ourselves, we are his people, and the sheep of his pasture" Psalm 100:3. Searching for yourself is to look deep inside yourself to see what God, the creator designed. Once you think it in the mind, then your thoughts create pictures, and your pictures have now become words that you speak out of your mouth. The Bible says in St. Matthew 12:34, "For out of the abundance of the heart the mouth speaketh". The mouth speaks what was created in the inside of the mind. It is not scripture but a true saying, "A mind is a terrible thing to waste." In order for the plan of God to be made manifest, we have to open up the creativeness deep down within ourselves. By allowing our hearts and mind to meditate and absorb the Word of God in our hearts and mind. "Let the words of my mouth, and the meditation of my heart, be acceptable in thy sight, O Lord, my strength, and my redeemer" Psalm 19:14.

Doubt causes the true plan of God to never come forth out of us; if we don't believe it, then we won't speak it. If we don't believe that God is able to perform what he placed in our life to be revealed to others, then we will not speak it out of our mouth, and if we don't speak it, it will not penetrate our life or anyone else's life. A word spoken in due season is like marrow to the bones. The Bible says in Proverbs 15:23, *A man hath joy by the answer of his mouth: and a word spoken in due season*, how good is it!

Aligning ourselves in the Word of God and the will of God is going to take some effort on our part. We can't align ourselves accordingly if we don't know ourselves.

Let's take a look at where and how it begins…

Life is created in a seed. The seed was created out of the dust of the ground. The seed that is called *man* was formed from the dust of the ground and was formed into what God called *man* and *woman*, they both created by God. This can be found in Genesis 1:27 that says, So *God created man in his own image, in the image of God created he him; male and female created he them.*

In God's process of creation, everything that was created was designed and aligned for the purpose, plan, and will of God. In this book, we will see the importance of staying in connection with the Father of all creation, and trust the process of his design for our life, and come to understand the importance of aligning ourselves with his word. Man fell from the will of God for his life by listening to the wrong voice that came from Satan. Eve is an example of following the devils lie as recorded in Genesis 3:1–6. Now the serpent was more subtil than any beast of the field which the LORD God had made. And he said unto the woman, Yea, hath God said, Ye shall not eat of every tree of the garden? And the woman said unto the serpent, We may eat of the fruit of the trees of the garden: but of the fruit of the tree which *is* in the midst of the garden, God hath said, Ye shall not eat of it, neither shall ye touch it, lest ye die. And the serpent said unto the woman, Ye shall not surely die: for God doth know that in the day ye eat thereof, then your eyes shall be opened, and ye shall be as gods, knowing good and evil. And when the woman saw that the tree *was* good for food, and that it *was* pleasant to the eyes, and a tree to be desired to make *one* wise, she took of the fruit thereof, and did eat, and gave also unto her husband with her; and he did eat. When we listen to the wrong voice of Satan and not the voice of God, it will causes our life to fall out of alignment with God's plan for our lives. Aligning ourselves back to the original plan of God and his creation is going to take some effort on our behalf. Here you will find some keys to help you in the process during our daily walk called *life*.

Keys/Steps to Alignment

I. WE MUST ACKNOWLEDGE AND RECOGNIZE OUR NEED FOR GOD'S HELP

To become aligned with Christ and his plan for our lives we must first acknowledge who Christ is and see the need for him in your life. If we never see the need for him, then we will never want to know him. Once you acknowledge Christ this is the first key to beginning the new process of alignment with Christ. One of the first steps in our scripture reference that will help us align ourselves with Christ, is to trust him completely with our lives. Proverbs 3:5–6, Trust in the LORD *with all thine heart; and lean not unto thine own understanding. In all thy ways acknowledge him, and he shall direct thy paths.*

II. ESTABLISHING WHY WE REALLY NEED HIM

We have to acknowledge that we are sinners. All have sin and come short of his glory Romans 3:23. We are not all that we thought we were, and we all have flaws and are in need of help so we can see God in peace. In Jeremiah 14:20, We acknowledge, O LORD, our wickedness, and the iniquity of our fathers: for we have sinned against thee. Psalm 32:5, I acknowledged my sin unto thee, and mine iniquity have I not hid. I said, I will confess my transgressions unto the LORD; and thou forgavest the iniquity of my sin. Once we acknowledge who God is, this establishes why we as a people need him. We acknowledge who God is and why you need him to lead our life.

This is a question that has been asked over and over again throughout each generation. Many times in life we find ourselves not knowing why we do certain things or why we go to certain places when we were told not to do so. Finally we end up disappointed, discouraged, or troubled. We think to ourselves, "I should have listened," or we say, "What is it that is in me that really wanted to do that anyway? Why, Lord, Why? Why me?" As we go through life and see the many things it brings, there is still this big question in the back of our mind. What if…what if I had done things differently, what if someone would have told me, what if I had talked to God first, what if I had just listened? Life is full of questions, and the only real answers can be founded in the Word of God. Yes, the BIBLE (God's Word), (B = Basic, I = Instructions, B = Before, L = Leaving, E = Earth)—the basic instructions before leaving earth. This is why we need God to help us in this life. The Bible teaches us in Psalm 46:1 that God is our refuge and strength, a very present help when we need him the most. God is our light; he is here to guide us throughout this process called life. The Bible says in Psalm 27:1, *The Lord is my light and my salvation; whom shall I fear? The Lord is the strength of my life; of whom shall I be afraid?* Psalm 119:105, Thy word is a lamp unto my feet, and a light unto my path.

Some of the benefits we gain by obeying and aligning ourselves to the Word of God is it will build us, strengthen us, help us, teach us, guide us, correct us, and most importantly the Word of God allows God to show us his Love he has for us. Life is full of ups and downs, good days and bad days, happy times and sad times. Having God there makes a difference in our lives. One thing that is truly for certain is the Word of God has answers to all our problems. Many books have been written to help with life issues and problems, and they all in some way or another lead us right back to the Word of God which gives us solutions for all the problems of mankind.

God is our *refuge and strength, a very present help in trouble.*
—Psalm 46:1

The Lord is my light and my salvation; whom shall I fear? The Lord is the strength of my life; of whom shall I be afraid? When the wicked, even mine enemies and my foes, came upon me to eat up my flesh, they stumbled and fell.
—Psalm 27:1–2

Howbeit when he, the Spirit of truth, is come, he will guide you into all truth: for he shall not speak of himself; but whatsoever he shall hear, that shall he speak: and he will shew you things to come.
—John 16:13

Not unto us, O Lord, not unto us, but unto thy name give glory, for thy mercy, and for thy truth's sake.
—Psalm 115:1

That ye may be the children of your Father which is in heaven: for he maketh his sun to rise on the evil and on the good, and sendeth rain on the just and on the unjust.
—Matthew 5:45

> *But thou shalt remember the Lord thy God: for it is he that giveth thee power to get wealth that he may establish his covenant which he sware unto thy fathers, as it is this day.*
>
> —Deuteronomy 8:18

> *Be not deceived; God is not mocked: for whatsoever a man soweth, that shall he also reap.*
>
> —Galatians 6:7

> *Go to the ant, thou sluggard; consider her ways, and be wise: Which having no guide, overseer, or ruler, Provideth her meat in the summer, and gathereth her food in the harvest.*
>
> —Proverbs 6:6–8

> *For the vision is yet for an appointed time, but at the end it shall speak, and not lie: though it tarry, wait for it; because it will surely come, it will not tarry.*
>
> —Habakkuk 2:3

Now that we have acknowledged him and have established why we need him, this leads you to step 3: let's learn of him. Jesus said, "Take my yoke upon you and learn of me, said the Lord." Matthew 11:28-30

III. BEGINNING TO LEARN OF HIM

One of the steps to learning how to align ourselves with Christ we must become teachable. Secondly, we must learn the behavior and conduct of Christ that requires studying the Word of God daily. In Matthew 11:28–30, Come unto me, all ye that labour and are heavy laden, and I will give you rest. Take my yoke upon you, and learn of me; for I am meek and lowly in heart: and ye shall find rest unto your souls. For my yoke *is* easy, and my burden is light. The yoke of Christ is the life he lived while on earth, Christ said for my yoke is easy, and my burden is light. Yoke is the joining of two animals together going in the same direction. In other words we have to connect to Christ and align ourselves together with him. To learn of Christ is to follow his patterns. We have to learn how to apply the Word of God to our lives. When we learn the true principle of God's Word and why we are here, we can have access to the true power of God and his life's principles and the true meaning and purpose of his dear son Jesus Christ. Once we put this into place, we can begin the alignment process by aligning ourselves according to the Word of God. To learn of Jesus plan and purpose for coming to earth Jesus was aligned with the fathers will and plan for his life. In 1 John 3:8 it gives us a reason why Jesus came, For this purpose the Son of God was manifested, that he might destroy the works of the devil. Once we learn and understand the purpose and will of Christ we begin to build a true foundation in our heart and mind of who God really is and why we exist and why the world exists and our purpose for being here on earth. We should pray and ask the Lord to help us align with his purpose and plan for our life. The Bible teaches us that the Word of God is line upon line, for precept must be upon precept, precept upon precept; line upon line, line upon line; here a little, and there a little, Isaiah 28:10. Learning the ways of Jesus always produce truth in our life, which allows us to learn his ways so we can follow his pattern in our lives. In St. John 14:6, Jesus said I am the way the truth and the life: no man cometh unto the Father, but by me. Jesus truth works effectively in our life so we can learn and practice his truth daily.

I Thessalonians 2:13, For this cause also thank we God without ceasing, because, when ye received the Word of God which ye heard of us, ye received it not as the word of men, but as it is in truth, the Word of God, which effectually worketh also in you that believe. *Our prayer should be as found in Psalm 86:11, teach me thy way, O Lord; I will walk in thy truth: unite my heart to fear thy name.*

One of the reason we should be persuaded and convince to learn and trust God Word is that our God can not lie, *God* is *not* a man, that he should *lie*; Neither the son of man, that he should repent: Hath he said, and shall he *not* do it? Or hath he spoken, and shall he *not make* it good, Numbers 23:19. Also in Hebrews 6:18 says, In that by two immutable things, in which *it was* impossible for God to lie, we might have a strong consolation. So shall my Word be that goeth forth out of my mouth: it shall not return unto me void, but it shall accomplish that which I please, and it shall prosper *in the thing* whereto I sent it. Isa. 55:11. Listen when I tell you, once we begin to trust and believe in God and his Word, the devil himself will come in any way he can to try to convince us that it's not true. Satan himself tried to deceive Jesus by misusing the scripture Psalm 91:11-12, and Jesus had to rebuke him so that he could stay in alignment with God's plan, will and purpose. This can be found in St. Matthew 4:1-11. This is how you know God is real and he is not like humans; *"He cannot lie, he cannot die, and nobody can beat him up,"* says Apostle David Billy Sr. One of the ways that we learn of

Jesus and align ourselves with him is by allowing him to lead us in the path of his righteousness, Psalm 23:3, He restoreth my soul: he leadeth me in *the paths of righteousness for his name's sake*. Once we establish the truth of God and learned about who he really is and our reason of existence here on earth, this will lead us to true repentance.

IV. REPENTANCE

Repentance is asking God for forgiveness for *all* of our sins, known and unknown. True repentance is asking God for forgiveness and never returning to that conduct or behavior in life again. Repentance should come from a broken, sincere and true heart. This is why it's good to be aware of our tongue and the words we speak, and always be mindful of our actions toward others on a daily basis.

No, it's not going to be all peaches and cream after that; everyone has an adversary—the devil, and he is going to try to draw us to himself or influence us to do the wrong thing he is on his job, which is to steal, kill, and destroy; St. John 10:10, and to try to take away all we have learned and to get us out of alignment with God and his dear son Jesus Christ. He comes to steal the word that we have learned of who God is and his plans for our life, he comes to kill the influence of those who has taught us the Word of God, and in the end, he will try to get us so distracted and away from God so he can have our soul and destroy it.

Therefore we should pray and ask the Lord to help us to say the right things, react in the right way and in the right manner, and show love according to his Word. Repentance is like changing the oil in a vehicle. We can only go so many miles before we need an oil change before the motor locks up and fall apart. We can only go so long without true repentance in our lives, therefore we have to go to God and ask him to clean up our lives through his Word. The benefits and rewards of true repentance is recorded in Acts 3:19, *Repent ye therefore, and be converted,* that your sins may be blotted out, when the times of refreshing shall come from the presence of the Lord; *Secondly,* True repentance produce true conversion in a person life. True repentance cause our sins to be *blotted out (removed or erase) lastly, true repentance allows us to experience a times of refreshing that shall come from the presence of the Lord.* True repentance gives us a heart of change which leads us to obedience.

> *Then Peter said unto them, Repent, and be baptized every one of you in the name of Jesus Christ for the remission of sins, and ye shall receive the gift of the Holy Ghost.*
>
> —Acts 2:38

> *I came not to call the righteous, but sinners to repentance.*
>
> —St. Luke 5:32

> *And saying, The time is fulfilled, and the kingdom of God is at hand: repent ye, and believe the gospel.*
>
> —St. Mark 1:15

Chapter 2

The Foundation Runs Deep
{Prayer Is Not an Option}

Why is a foundation required for our life? The foundation sets a solid base for what your trying to build and how stable and permanent it will be when it is finished. Not all foundations are built the same, nor are they all made up of the same materials. Foundations are built according to the climate in which you live. When we give our life to the Lord, he begins laying a new foundation in us that will be unshakable. This is why he must lay a new foundation in us that will run deep down within the core of our life. Because Satan, the god of this world, has blinded the minds of the people so they won't believe the truth of God's Word; as it is recorded in II Corinthians 4:4; in whom the god of this world hath blinded the minds of them which believe not, lest the light of the glorious gospel of Christ, who is the image of God, should shine unto them. The deeper the foundation, the more solid and permanent and firm durable the structure will be. The deeper we allow God to go into our life, the more of ourselves he removes and the more of himself he sets in place. Once we allow God into our hearts, he will begin the alignment process. When God created us, how did we get out of alignment? We got out of alignment with God through disobeying his instructions for building our lives and then we begin to act upon our own thoughts and do what we wanted to do that is not according to God's blue prints for our lives. Praying to God and asking for his directions has now become unclear and the blueprint is fainted.

It started in creation when Eve allowed the serpent to deceive her into eating the forbidden fruit, and then Adam received of the fruit from Eve that was told by God not to eat of it; you can read this in Genesis 2:16–17; And the LORD God commanded the man, saying, Of every tree of the garden thou mayest freely eat: but of the tree of the knowledge of good and evil, thou shalt not eat of it: for in the day that thou eatest thereof thou shalt surely die. Genesis 3:1–19, Now the serpent was more subtil than any beast of the field which the LORD God had made. And he said unto the woman, Yea, hath God said, ye shall not eat of every tree of the garden? And the woman said unto the serpent, we may eat of the fruit of the trees of the garden: but of the fruit of the tree which *is* in the midst of the garden, God hath said, ye shall not eat of it, neither shall ye touch it, lest ye die. And the serpent said unto the woman, ye shall not surely die: for God doth know that in the day ye eat thereof, then your eyes shall be opened, and ye shall be as gods, knowing good and evil. And when the woman saw that the tree *was* good for food, and that it *was* pleasant to the eyes, and a tree to be desired to make *one* wise, she took of the fruit thereof, and did eat, and gave also unto her husband with her; and he did eat. And the eyes of them both were opened, and they knew that they *were* naked; and they sewed fig leaves together, and made themselves aprons. And they heard the voice of the LORD God walking in the garden in the cool of the day: and Adam and his wife hid themselves from the presence of the LORD God amongst the trees of the garden. And the LORD God called unto Adam, and said unto him, Where *art* thou? And he said, I heard thy voice in the garden, and I was afraid, because I *was* naked; and I hid myself. And he said, Who told thee that thou *wast* naked? Hast thou eaten of the tree, whereof I commanded thee that thou shouldest not eat? And the man said, The woman whom thou gavest *to be* with me, she gave me of the tree, and I did eat. And the LORD God said unto the woman, What *is* this *that* thou hast done? And the woman said, The serpent beguiled me, and I did eat. And the LORD God said unto the serpent, Because thou hast done this, thou *art* cursed above all cattle, and above every beast of the field; upon thy belly shalt thou go, and dust shalt thou eat all the days of thy life: and I will put enmity between thee and the woman, and between thy seed and her seed; it shall bruise thy head, and thou shalt bruise his heel. Unto the woman he said, I will greatly multiply thy sorrow and thy conception; in sorrow thou shalt bring forth children; and thy desire *shall be* to thy husband, and he shall rule over thee. And unto Adam he said, Because thou hast hearkened unto the voice of thy wife, and hast eaten of the tree, of which I commanded thee, saying, Thou shalt not eat of it: cursed *is* the ground for thy sake; in sorrow shalt thou eat *of* it all the days of thy life; thorns also and thistles shall it bring forth to thee; and thou shalt eat the herb of the field; in the sweat of thy face shalt thou eat bread, till thou return unto the ground; for out of it wast thou taken: for dust thou *art*, and unto dust shalt thou return.

Every house is built on a foundation, but not every house is built on the same type of foundation, a house built on an unstable foundation can have a number of serious problems, so it is in the natural so it is in the spirit. In others words, God builds us all differently because of the different assignments and plans he has for us. Nevertheless, we all must allow him to build us in a way where we want be shakable or unstable to carry out his will, plan and purpose for our lives. The purpose of all foundations is to transmit the load (weight) of the house that's being built. God builds us as individuals according to the weight of our assignment. The bible teaches us in Psalm 127:1, *Except the LORD* build *the house,* they labour in vain that build it. Jeremiah 29:11, For I know *the* thoughts that I think toward you, saith *the* LORD, thoughts of peace, and not of evil, to *give* you an expected end. We as individuals were created in God's image but yet our assignments are not the same. Building a strong foundation in God requires spending quality time in prayer and studying God's Word and allowing his Word to move us in the right direction. When we allow God to build our house we can rest assure the right and true foundation will be laid. Dig your spiritual foundation deep; develop deep faith. Building a sure spiritual foundation means praying, investing time in his word, inspecting (keeping your life in check), and ensuring the foundation is maintained—and God's given us the instructions to do this through his Word. When we build on a firm foundation of Christ, we can withstand whatever comes our way and God will set his approval upon our lives. In II Timothy 2:19 the Bible tells us, Nevertheless the foundation of God standeth sure, having this seal, The Lord knoweth them that are his. And, let every one that nameth the name of Christ depart from iniquity.

When the Lord builds our life, it is vitally important that we obey what he require of us, we can find a prime example of how Christ builds us and gives us an example in foundations always require digging deep. In St. Luke 6:46-49 And why call ye me, Lord, Lord, and do not the things which I say? Whosoever cometh to me, and heareth my sayings, and doeth them, I will shew you to whom he is like: He is like a man which built an house, and digged deep, and laid the foundation on a rock: and when the flood arose, the stream beat vehemently upon that house, and could not shake it: for it was founded upon a rock. But he that heareth, and doeth not, is like a man that without a foundation built an house upon the earth; against which the stream did beat vehemently, and immediately it fell; and the ruin of that house was great.

The true foundation goes down deep, removes all hidden debris, and becomes leveled out so that a fresh layer of concrete can be laid. The Word of God is solid fresh concrete that is laid in our lives, The Bible says, in II Corinthians 5:17, Therefore if any man be in Christ, he is a new creature: old things are passed away; behold, all things are become new. When we obey his Words our heart is open and receptive and ready to be cleansed, when we disobey his Word our lives will remain incomplete and closed which will eventually come to ruin.

The Word of God is now understood in a better manner. The foundation of God is being embedded into our hearts and minds. We have to make sure our thoughts and our desires are aligned according to the plan and will of God. It is vitally important to understand that obedience to God produces a deep cleansing of ourselves in his Word.

The Word of God will clean us up and allow a new foundation to be laid in our life. The old way of thinking in this life will be removed, and the newness of his life will be laid in us. God wants to lay a new foundation that will transform our life. We must allow him to dig out all the dirt of our old thinking and life style and lay a new foundation so our lives can be in alignment with him. He wants to establish a foundation of repentance and true holiness deep down inside of us. Take God at his Word, the Bible says in, Acts 3:19, Repent ye therefore, and be converted, that your sins may be blotted out, when the times of refreshing shall come from the presence of the Lord. I Peter 1:13-16, Wherefore gird up the loins of your mind, be sober, and hope to the end for the grace that is to be brought unto you at the revelation of Jesus Christ; as obedient children, not fashioning yourselves according to the former lusts in your ignorance: but as he which hath called you is holy, so be ye holy in all manner of conversation; because it is written, Be ye holy; for I am holy.

Prayer Is Not an Option

The Lord gives us a required mandate to pray always. I Thessalonians 5:17 says, Pray without ceasing. In St. Luke 18:1 says, And he spake a parable unto them to this end, that men ought always to pray, and not to faint.

Prayer is like oxygen without it we will die spiritually, and immediately be cut off from God. When we as a people pray, it opens up our spiritual air passage way so we can breathe, while we are talking to our heavenly father and we are in communication with the God of all creation about what his plan is for us, and what assignment he has designed for us to carry out while here on earth.

Our lifeline is prayer; which is the blueprint for our life. Prayer will help you press beyond our feelings and emotions. All we have to do is trust, believe, and walk in his divine plan. Stay connected to the vine. Stay in alignment with what he has promised because he will perform it. What God has promised, he is also able to perform. Romans 4:21 states, And being fully persuaded that, what he had promised, he was *able also to perform.*

The key to unlocking every question in your mind or thoughts is in prayer. Prayer is not an event that takes place here and there; it is a lifestyle for everyday living. Prayer is the plumb line to our life and the foundation on which we stand. Having a transformational quiet time in prayer is not an issue of being spiritual enough. Rather, it is an issue of spiritually preparing the mind and heart to follow God.

- Prayer can succeed where other means have failed: 1 Kings 18:20–39.

- Prayer should never be our last resort but our first response: 1 Thessalonians 5:17, Philippians 4:6–7.

- Prayer fulfills mental and emotional needs; we were made to function best mentally and emotionally in a prayerful relationship with God: Psalm 17:8–9, St. John 14:27, III John 1:2, Isaiah 54:17.

- Prayer grants us the privilege of experiencing God: Philippians 3:10, Jeremiah 29:11, Psalm 139:23, Joshua 1:9, Proverbs 3:7, Psalm 27:4.

- Prayer makes our experience with God more real on a mental and emotional level: Mark 1:35–39 (AMP), Colossians 3:1–2 (NIV).

- Prayer keeps us humble: Proverbs 11:2, 22:4; Micah 6:8; James 4:10.

- Prayer is always in order and available; nothing can keep us from approaching God in prayer except our own choices: Psalm 139:7-10, Romans 8:38–39.

- Prayer is always in season, never an option; even Jesus prayed: Matthew 26:39–42.

When we sum it up, prayer is the true plumb line, the lifeline to our creator, God himself.

This is what prayer does:

Prayer gives us power to conquer the enemy,

Readiness to do God's will,

Anointing to win every battle,

Yokes will be destroyed,

Effectiveness to produce, elevation for promotion,

Restoration from the hurts and things of our past.

This is why *prayer* is essential. Not because we have it all together, but because we need God's help so we can get it all together!

Chapter 3

Trusting the Process {Studying God's Word, Not an Option}

Trusting God and studying the Word of God and allowing the Word to be rooted and grounded in our life are two of the most important things in this spiritual walk with Christ. In order to trust God, we must first know God.

> *Trust in the LORD with all thine heart; and lean not unto thine own understanding. In all thy ways acknowledge him, and he shall direct thy paths.*
>
> —Proverbs 3:5–6

To know God, we must study him. Before we put our trust in anyone, we have to learn of them and find out who they are, what they have to offer, and what they can do to help improve our life. In other words, what can they bring to the table? Are they going to be an asset or a liability?

> Study to shew *thyself approved unto God, a workman that needeth not* to *be ashamed, rightly dividing the word of truth.*
>
> —2 Timothy 2:15

Trusting God is not a matter of when or if we need him; it's a matter of needing him in the entire process called life. As we walk through this life, we will always find the need to trust in someone or something, so why not trust your creator. Putting our trust in our creator God almighty, is like putting our vehicle into the hands of the maker of that design. When our vehicle gets out of alignment, our first thought is to take it back to the dealer who manufactured the vehicle to place it back into the position where it needs to be. But because of so many shops that have come up since our vehicle was designed, you don't know exactly where to take it for the best care. So now you have to decide whether you're going to put your trust in this secondary shop or going to put your trust and finances in the hands of the dealer who designed the vehicle. Trust is the key factor here; as it is in the natural, so it is in the spirit. When you find yourself in places of uncertainties and you're trying to find your way through this process called life, look into the owner's manual, begin to search the book, start to study the book; God's Word is true, and it has proved itself over and over again.

> ***Commit*** thy *works unto the Lord, and* thy *thoughts shall be established.*-+
>
> —Proverbs 16:3

> *This book of the law shall not depart out of thy mouth; but thou shalt meditate therein day and night, that thou mayest observe to do according to all that is written therein: for then thou shalt make thy way prosperous, and then thou shalt have good success.*
>
> —Joshua 1:8

Learning to trust God involves knowing God's Word, because God speaks to us through his Word. Noah knew the voice of God and he was found righteous unto him. In Genesis 6:13, 22, And God said unto Noah, The end of all flesh is come before me; for the earth is filled with violence through them; and, behold, I will destroy them with the earth. Thus did Noah; according to all that God commanded him, so did he. Noah nor anyone had ever seen rain before, but Noah knew and he followed the voice of God, and he moved when God spoke. When we begin to study the Word of God, we will come to know his voice even if we don't always understand what he is doing. We can begin to follow God's voice by saying, "Lord, I trust you even when I can't trace you." Lord, teach us to know your voice and to act upon it when we hear it. In St. John 10:27–28, Jesus says, My sheep hear my voice, and I know them, and they follow me: And I give unto them eternal life; and they shall never perish, neither shall any man pluck them out of my hand.

Putting your trust in someone you don't know is not as easy as it seems. Your heart will begin to be filled with doubt and disbelief and most of all fear. When you begin to search the Word and study the life of God and our Lord Jesus Christ, we will come to know him for ourselves, and love and trust will fill our heart. In I John 4:18, it says, There is no *fear [false evidence appearing real]* in *love*; but *perfect love* casteth *out fear*; because *fear [false evidence appearing* _real]_ hath torment. He that feareth is not made _perfect_ in _love_. Perfect love involves trusting, obeying and keeping God commandments. In St. John 14:15 Jesus said, if ye love me, keep my commandments. II Corinthians 13:11, Finally, brethren, farewell. Be _perfect_, be of _good_ comfort, be of one mind, live in peace; and the God of _love_ and peace shall be with you.

In order to trust, obey and follow God's voice we must get an understanding of who he is and why he has called us for his plan and purpose. In prayer God is always available to help us understand his Word, plan and purpose for our lives as we realize how much we need him. We can always take the time in prayer to acknowledge him and why we need him and help us to learn of him as we lay a true foundation and study his word. We can always repent and ask him to remove all things in our lives that are not of him. We can ask him to teach us to accept his plan and will for our lives. We can ask him to help us follow his leading and steps so that our lives may flow as the Bible says. When we acknowledge him in all of our ways he is always there to direct our path.

When we study the Word of God, we are learning who God is, why we were created, and why it's so important to live by the words that have proceeded out of the mouth of God. Studying and trusting him brings us closer to him; and we begin to understand and trust him more and more.

> Wisdom is the _principal_ thing; _therefore get_ wisdom:
> and with all thy getting get understanding.
>
> —Proverbs 4:7

*Trust in the LORD with all thine heart; And
lean not unto thine own understanding.*

—Proverbs 3:5

*But he answered and said, It is written,
Man shall not live by bread alone, but
by every word that proceedeth out of the mouth of God.*

—St. Matthew 4:4

Chapter 4

The Orchestrating Process

Many times God will orchestrate and arrange our lives in ways we don't totally and completely understand due to our carnal and natural mind. This is why we must learn how to walk and live by faith and not by sight. The Bible describes in, II Corinthians 5:7, for we walk by faith, not by sight. In the Word of God Faith is described in Hebrews 11:1 Now faith is the substance of things hoped for, the evidence of things not seen. Our natural sight is the enemy or opposite of walking by faith, because faith comes by hearing and hearing the Word of God, Romans 10:17. Notice faith gives us evidence of the things not seen to our natural eye sight.

God is moving and opening doors every day, but it's up to us by faith to walk through them. When God closes a door, it's for our protection; when God opens a door, it's for our benefit to grow and develop in him. God is investing time in us and giving us opportunities to trust him even more. When the doors of opportunity are opened by God, no man can shut them; only we can shut the door by not walking through it and saying, "No, I'll wait." Trust me when I say, "Oh, I know very well how we can miss out on opportunities from God."

This is why it's very important to know the voice of God and move when he says to move.

Our adversary the devil is like a roaring lion seeking whom he may destroy; he doesn't want us to do God's will. In I Peter 5:8 it says, Be sober, be vigilant; because your adversary the *devil, as a roaring lion*, walketh about, *seeking whom he may devour*. For every door that God opens for us, the enemy will try to trick us and detour us from walking through it; he'll tell us to walk through a different door, or say stay in the place where you are. Moving out of comfortable place is either going to make us or break us. However, God is calling us to step out our comfort zones and walk by faith and experience his super natural power, authority and ability for our life, unless we will become a target for the enemy to devour and destroy our lives.

Every decision we make in life has a benefit or consequence; this is why it's imperative to ask God to direct our lives daily.

Trust in the LORD with all thine heart;
And lean not unto thine own understanding.
In all thy ways acknowledge him, And he shall direct thy paths.

—Proverbs 3:5-6

Now God himself and our Father, and our Lord
Jesus Christ, direct our way unto you.

—I Thessalonians 3:11

Daily prayer and being in communication with our Lord Jesus Christ are key. This is why we should pray, Lord, deliver me from me (the enemy in me and my self-will). We can't ask God for more and be afraid to step out and receive more. We can't be afraid of people, about what they will say or what they will do, no matter who the people are, we must learn to listen to the voice of God. Some people can have our best interest at heart and help guide us through the word of God toward the right path for our life. However others may say they have us, but try to hold us back because they lack the qualities we have and they will try to discourage us from the decisions we make for our life. Never allow other people to make us miss out on the opportunities God has for our life.

An example of not allowing other people to detour us from God's orchestrated plans for our lives is demonstrated in the life of Jesus Christ. God's orchestrated plan for Jesus was to die for the sins of mankind, and he didn't allow anyone to detour him from that purpose. Jesus finished the purpose and plan that God had for his life,

St. John 19:30, When Jesus therefore had received the vinegar, he said, It is finished: and he bowed his head, and gave up the ghost.

In spite of what people are saying, finish the course and stay in alignment with the will and plan that God has for our life. Allow God to orchestrate your life. Don't depend on others to carry out the assignment or vision God gave to you. Others can help, but we must walk and carry out the vision, plan, and purpose God has called us to do. We alone will have to stand before God by ourselves for what we were designed and created to do by God and not others.

Another keys to aligning ourselves to God and his Word is obedience. However obeying the Word of God and his voice is not always easy, because of our sinful natural. In Galatians 5:17 it says, For *the flesh* lusteth *against the Spirit*, and *the Spirit against the flesh*: and these are contrary *the* one to *the* other: so that ye cannot do *the* things that ye would. Obedience to God is not just doing what you think is important or only doing what you think is safe. Obedience is pressing beyond the hard stuff, going against what you feel, and allowing the

Word of God to process you to become a better you, a true child of God and a believer of his promises.

When God is taking us through the alignment process, he is orchestrating our life. When we allow God to move on our behalf, things will begin to line up, and we give God something to work with. No, this process is not all peaches and cream, but yes, it will straighten up and align our life. Aligning ourselves is getting us out of the way and allowing God to have his way. The Bible teaches us in Proverbs 14:14, The backslider in heart shall be filled with his own ways: and a good man shall be satisfied from himself. It says in II Corinthians 12:9–10, *My grace is sufficient for thee: for my strength is made perfect in weakness. Most gladly therefore will I rather glory in my infirmities, that the power of Christ may rest upon me. Therefore I take pleasure in infirmities, in* reproaches, in necessities, in persecutions, in distresses for Christ's sake: for when I am weak, then am I strong. Then in Jeremiah 29:11 the Lord says, For I know the thoughts that I think toward you, saith the LORD, thoughts of peace, and not of evil, to give you an expected end.

The Word of God was designed with us in mind, and the enemy doesn't want us to learn the Word, rehearse the Word, or apply it to your life. It's all in aligning ourselves going through the process, and allowing God to orchestrate our life. In walking through the process, we must allow ourselves to listen and hear the voice of God. To hear is one thing, but to really listen is totally different. When you hear someone talking, you don't necessarily move. When you are really listing to what is being said, you are paying attention and you will act upon what they say and began to move differently.

As we align our lives with God and his Word, God will orchestrate and guided our life to speak into others' lives and encourage them to keep fighting this good fight of faith and to learn to trust

God in the process of whatever they are faced with. One day God had me to call a friend of mine, not knowing what all my friend was going through; he had me call to call and minister to them. God told me to call my friend and tell them to bring their spouse to church on a particular Sunday. Now, I was in the midst of working on a project when God spoke to me and told me to gather some young men who who grew up in our church, and began to invite them all to come back and receive an impartation from our Apostle and Pastor as to what God is getting ready to do in this new season. Those who would respond to the invitation and come I know would be blessed as a result of attending the service. In the process of me talking to my friend and telling them what I heard God say to me concerning them as my friends, I told my friend that God said if your spouse wants to be delivered and healed from what they are going through, they will come. Not knowing the issues of the true matter at hand, my friend told the spouse what I said. The next couple of days, I talked to my friend, and my friend ensured me the spouse would be there but was a little frightened about why they needed to come on that particular Sunday. So I reiterated to them what God had spoken to me to tell them prior to us talking that day.

As I waited to see what God was going to do on that coming Sunday with me gathering the men together and speaking with my friend as well, the anticipation was growing in my heart and spirit.

Five days of waiting before the next service and also since I had spoken to my friend, come Sunday morning, my friend and their spouse showed up at church. A lot of the young men and others I had invited came, and church was lit (as this generation would say); the service was on fire, and the Spirit of God moved in our midst that day. I took the spouse of my friend by the hand and we came down to the altar, and as we were there, I heard the Spirit of God say, "Lay your hand them and begin to intercede in the spirit." As I procrastinated at first because our Apostle was so on fire that day, God spoke again and said, "Lay your hands on them," and as I laid my hands, the Spirit of God began to move and the tears began to flow and the cry out of deliverance was now taking place. As God was sending forth his healing virtue, one of the young men I had invited came to the altar, gave his life to the Lord, and rejoined the church; he had not been there since he was a teenager That's just like God working simultaneously on both ends of the alter. When we allow God to orchestrate our lives and act upon his voice when he speak to us things will fall into place even if we can't see at the time, it's working inside of the process. After speaking with the young man and all those who had come that day for service, I began to talk to my friends spouse just reassured them of what God had just done on that day. We prayed again, and as we touched and agreed, God continued to move again and again, as they were reassured it was nobody but God.

When we allow ourselves to hear the voice of God and move and do what he say to do, The Orchestrating Process is now being made manifested in our lives. God's plans will overtake our own thoughts and his Word is made alive. In the mist of going through this particular situation God began to reveal this to me. Going through the process of aligning ourselves with the Word of God and doing what is required of us is like walking down a long hallway by ourselves or walking down the runway to get on an airplane for the first time; the anticipation and anxiety is super high and we don't know what to expect, but we do know something is there and can't wait to get there. Working the process is what most people don't want to do because it takes time—"the waiting period." We live in a society where people want everything quick, fast, and in a hurry, like right now—whatever we want, have it right now. In the midst of the waiting period is when prayer comes into play. Not just prayer but *trust* and *belief.* Are you really trusting and believing in the voice and the Word of God, or are you going through the motions? When you align yourself to listen to God and believe his Word and walk out the calling, the revelation of his Word and plan for our life is made manifest.

Aligning ourselves with the Word of God and his will for us only comes when we spend time with him. Prayer is the number one key in the *alignment process.* It is our lifeline (plumb line to keep our foundation and building in order). If we don't pray and talk to God, we cannot know the will or plan of God. Some may say we don't need to pray; prayer is a myth, God knows my heart. Those thoughts are of the devil, the wicked one Satan himself. Yes, God knows our heart; that's why he told us to pray because the condition of our heart needs to be changed and alignment to his heart, not your own. The Bible teaches us in Jeremiah 17:9, The *heart is deceitful above all* things, *and desp*erately wicked: who can know it. Psalm 51:10 says, Create in me a *clean heart,* O God; And renew *a* right *spirit* within *me.*

Men ought always to pray, and not to faint.

—St. Luke 18:1

Praying always with all prayer and supplication in the Spirit, and watching thereunto with all perseverance and supplication for all saints.

—Ephesians 6:18

Evening, and morning, and at noon, will I pray, *and cry aloud: and he shall hear my voice.*

—Psalms 55:17

A few days later, I received the testimony of what God had done for my friends spouse from that Sunday. I prayed to God, "Let me hear your voice and move the first time you speak." Prayer and believing God are essential, and without them, we would fail. Hebrews 11:6, But without faith it is *impossible to please him: for he that cometh to God must believe that he is, and that he is a rewarder of them that diligently seek him.* James 5:15, And *the prayer of faith shall save the sick, and the* Lord shall raise him up; and if he have committed sins, they shall be forgiven him.

When we get into alignment with what God is telling us to do, things will begin to work together for our good. Healing, deliverance, wholeness, faith, hope, love, and charity and all of the fruit of the Spirit will begin to be produced in our life. A couple of questions I often ask are, "Can people eat from my tree (life)?" and "Is my life an example of what God's Word looks like?" These questions are the very tools we must live by when we are walking with God, and they help keep us in alignment and in communication through prayer with our Lord and Savior Jesus Christ. The Bible teaches us in II Corinthians 3:2, Ye are our *epistle written in our hearts, known and read of all men.* St. Matthew 7:16, Ye shall *know them by their fruits.* Our Lord and Savior Jesus Christ will orchestrate our life in such a way that we will begin to see how *all* things in this life must be in alignment with him even when we don't want them to. We as people tend to want things our own way, but we must trust and believe in God's will to be done and fulfilled in us.

Must Jesus bear this cross alone and all the world go free? No, there is a cross for everyone to bear. St. Matthew 16:24, Then said Jesus unto his disciples, If any man will come after me, let him deny himself, and take up his cross, and follow me.

Things are placed in alignment for a reason. When it is out of place, the flow is off and things become difficult to work with and work through. When the alignment is off, it doesn't run well; it will pull us to the left or the right, and we are no longer right in the middle where we belong. Our vision is faded and out of focus. The Bible teaches us in Deuteronomy 5:32, Ye shall observe *to do therefore as the Lord your God hath commanded you: ye shall not turn aside to the right hand or to the left.* In St. Matthew 7:13–14 it says, Enter ye in at *the strait gate*: for wide *is the gate*, and broad *is the* way, that leadeth to destruction, and many there be which go in threat: Because strait *is the gate*, and narrow *is the way, which leadeth unto life, and few there be that find it.*

When the vehicle's wheels are out of alignment, the vehicle will begin to pull to one side and cause the steering wheel to be hard to adjust. When your vehicle's wheels aren't properly aligned, it can cause your tires to wear very quickly or unevenly. We may even notice that our steering wheel may pull to one direction or another. Bad alignment can also cause our steering wheel to shake and vibrate, which over time can make driving very uncomfortable. Your love walk with Christ Jesus is no different; when we are out of alignment, it causes our life to be uneven or out of balance and hard to adjust and very uncomfortable. Things in the body of Christ don't seem to be moving in the right direction. Everything we plan seems to fail; our programs are not working, our assignments aren't lining up, and now the flow of our personal ministry doesn't seem to be working in the way that it ought to. This is why *prayer* is vitally important and essential to be done daily. Prayer is our lifeline (plumb line). Reading the Word of God (our mason line or chalk line) daily is what carries us through day to day. When we apply the Word of God to our life daily, it will guide our life every step of the way.

> The Bible teaches us that God will never leave us, nor will he forsake us. Let your conversation be without covetousness; and be content with such things as ye have: for he hath said, I will never leave thee, nor forsake thee.
>
> —Hebrews 13:5

> Peace I leave with you, my peace I give unto you: not as the world giveth, give I unto you. Let not your heart be troubled, neither let it be afraid.
>
> —John 14:27

> I will not leave you comfortless: I will come to you.
>
> —John 14:18

> Because thou hast kept the word of my patience, I also will keep thee from the hour of temptation, which shall come upon all the world, to try them that dwell upon the earth.
>
> —Revelation 3:10

> Thy words were found, and I did eat them; and thy word was unto me the joy and rejoicing of mine heart: for I am called by thy name, O Lord God of hosts.
>
> —Jeremiah 15:16

Total alignment with God and his Word will cause your life to be fulfilled, and the growing process will be phenomenal. We shall be like a tree planted by the rivers of water, ever increasing and becoming all that God has arranged and planned for our life. Psalm 1:3 says, And he shall be like a tree planted *by the rivers of water, that bringeth forth his fruit in his season; his leaf also shall not wither; and whatsoever he doeth shall prosper.*

Your roots are planted so deeply in God that when things seem to try to bring discouragement and you don't see the manifestation yet of what God has promised, your roots will begin to bud and bring forth fruit. Job 14:9 says, Yet through *the scent of water* it will bud, and bring forth boughs like *a* plant. Don't allow anyone or anything to discourage you; no matter how long it takes, God will perform his Word in our life and it will come to pass. In Romans 4:20–21 says, Abraham staggered not at the promise of God through unbelief; but was strong in faith, giving glory to God; And being fully persuaded that, what he had promised, he was able also to perform.

Trusting without seeing is part of the process. When we are on our job or planning the outcome of our business, we trust that at the end of the day or the end of the week we will have enough revenue come in for us to pay our employees and more than enough to pay ourselves and to keep our business afloat. Trusting God and allowing him to orchestrate our life through it all is aligning our will to his will, reminding him of his Word, by asking God to let his will be done in earth as it is being done in heaven St. Matt. 6:10. What may seem impossible to man God uses the impossible to prove and give evidence that God is real. In the realness of his very essence, God will manifest himself and touch us with his presence like no one has ever touched us before. The evidence and proof of his touch you will experience His peace, rest, and calmness to the point where you will ask the Lord to do it again and again."

Whenever God touches us again and again this is because he is helping us to arrange and orchestrate our lives to be in harmony with his plan and purpose for our lives. Align yourself with God, trust in him, trust the plan, and trust the process.

> *The Lord directs the steps of the godly. He delights in every detail of their lives. Though they stumble, they will never fall, for the Lord holds them by the hand.*
>
> —Psalm 37:23-24 (NLT)

> *We can make our plans, but the Lord determines our steps.*
>
> —Proverbs 16:9 (NLT)

Chapter 5

The Shifting Process

When we drifting out of alignment from what God had designed for our lives, causes God to shift what he called you to do to someone else, and this can cause us to miss Gods plans and purpose for our lives. In other words, when we are out of place because of a wrong decision we made, it will not change God's plans, but it will change our outcome. Let's take a look into God's Word and see why it is very important to stay in step with what was designed because wrong decisions will alter the outcome of our life. Let's look into the life of Esau and Jacob. In Genesis 25:23 (NIV) we read where, The Lord *said to Rachael*, "Two nations are in your womb, and two peoples from within you will be separated; one people will be stronger than the other, and the older will serve the younger."

Based on the scriptures recorded in Genesis 25:19–34. In biblical history the firstborn son is the one to inherit the promise of the father, and the inheritance will pass on to him regardless of how many sons he had. The firstborn inherited the leadership of the family and the judicial authority of his father and would receive the most financially and so on. As the eldest son of Isaac, Esau should have inherited the covenant with God that Abraham had passed on to Isaac, but Esau didn't fully value the importance of the birthright (inheritance). Because he was not focused on his commitment to his birthright, he allowed his hunger for natural food to cause him to forfeit the value of the birthright, he traded it to his younger brother, Jacob, for a "mess of food" (a meal of stew) when he was too hungry to consider what he was throwing away. Esau allowed one little meal to shift his entire life from inheriting his birthright.

When you step out of alignment, there is a shifting that takes place. Just as when your vehicle is knocked out of alignment, the wheels begin to shift toward a different direction. This causes things to move outside of the original plan and design. Now Jacob, who knew the importance of the birthright and may have envied it because he was second in line instead of being first, maneuver and tricked his way into position to gain the birthright. One thing you have to remember in life when you are in alignment with God the father of creation and your parents in the natural, there is always someone observing you to see the outcome of your decisions. Therefore the other person may say, because of their bad decisions we can make good decisions to gain what they have lost. The enemy is always lurking to see if we really value the position or place that we are in. It's imperative that we stay in alignment with the father. Aligning ourselves with the plan and will of God is very important; this way we will stay in step with his will. Is it an easy task? Of course not. It requires movement on our behalf, praying to God on a daily basis, learning to use the keys and the tools that are needed, allows God to align and orchestrate our lives according to his plan and purpose.

God's Word has always proven to be true, and God will back up his word even if it means using someone else in place of us. The

Bible says in Isaiah 55:11, So shall my *word be that goeth forth out of my mouth: it shall not return unto me void, but it shall accomplish that which I please, and it shall prosper in the thing whereto I sent it.* In Psalm 89:34, My covenant will I not break, nor alter the thing that is gone out of my lips.

Staying focused on God in the midst of our assignment is very hard. God will call us to an assignment in different seasons to see if we really trust him. The different assignments from God do not change the purpose of God in our life. God created each and every one of us for a plan and a purpose. This is why it is so important that we get in place with God, so we will know the purpose for our lives. Shifting our assignment will cost us something; ask Esau and Jacob. We will pay by doing things that God has not designed for us and the ones who envy us and took what we had will pay the cost to keep it. Yes, God gives grace and mercy every day, but it also alters where God wants to accomplish in our life. It will cause God to move differently. This is clearly why the Bible teaches us in Isaiah 55: 8–9, For my thoughts are not your thoughts, neither are your ways my ways, saith the LORD. For as the heavens are higher than the earth, so are my ways higher than your ways, and my thoughts than your thoughts.

The plan and design he had for us has now been shifted; God still needs to fulfill his work, so he will use someone else. In the midst of him using another vessel, we are now questioning God for using someone else when we know deep down inside it should have been us. Because of this shift we are now living with regret wishing we have submitted to Gods process for our life at the time he wanted to use us. Jesus was assigned the hardest task of all, which involved dyeing for all the sins of mankind, and his last words before yielding up his spirit back to God was, "*It is finished*" St. John 19:30. Jesus could have stopped once he realized what crucifixion really consisted of, St.

Matthew 26:38–39, Then saith he unto them, My soul is exceeding sorrowful, even unto death: tarry ye here, and watch with me. And he went a little farther, and fell on his face, and prayed, saying, O my Father, if it be possible, let this cup pass from me: nevertheless not as I will, but as thou wilt.

Prayer will help us press beyond our feelings and emotions. Jesus is touched by the feeling of our infirmities. We must learn to trust, believe, and walk in his divine plan, and stay connected to Jesus as the vine, St. John 15:1-7, I am the true vine, and my Father is the husbandman. Every branch in me that beareth not fruit he taketh away: and every *branch* that beareth fruit, he purgeth it, that it may bring forth more fruit. Now ye are clean through the word which I have spoken unto you. Abide in me, and I in you. As the branch cannot bear fruit of itself, except it abide in the vine; no more can ye, except ye abide in me. I am the vine, ye *are* the branches: He that abideth in me, and I in him, the same bringeth forth much fruit: for without me ye can do nothing. If a man abide not in me, he is cast forth as a branch, and is withered; and men gather them, and cast *them* into the fire, and they are burned. If ye abide in me, and my words abide in you, ye shall ask what ye will, and it shall be done unto you. We must stay in alignment with what he has promised us because he will perform it, Romans 4:20-21, He staggered not at the promise of God through unbelief; but was strong in faith, giving glory to God; and being fully persuaded that, what he had promised, he was able also to perform. For in Hebrews 4:15–16 it states , For we have not an high priest which cannot be touched with the feeling of our infirmities; but was in all points tempted like as we are, yet without sin. Therefore come boldly unto the throne of grace that we may obtain mercy, and find grace to help in time of need.

He staggered not at the promise of God through unbelief; but was strong in faith, giving glory to God; And being fully persuaded that, what he had promised, he was able also to perform.

—Romans 4:20

We have to align ourselves according to God's plan. When we step out of alignment, it causes a shifting to take place not just in our life, but also in the life of the person God is now using to do what he had called us to do. As a matter of fact, abandoning your assignment shows lack of commitment, honor, and trust for God. Esau at the time could not see beyond his belly and trust it cost him more than he was expecting. In Hebrew 12:16-17 we find where it says of Esau, lest there *be* any fornicator, or profane person, as Esau, who for one morsel of meat sold his birthright. For ye know how that afterward, when he would have inherited the blessing, he was rejected: for he found no place of repentance, though he sought it carefully with tears. The enemy will have your mind so clouded by what our flesh wants, he won't allow us to see that our birthright to the kingdom of heaven is worth far more than what our flesh has to offer. We must crave and long for the things of God more than food, success, money, or fame, because our hunger and desire for the things of God will keep us in alignment with his plan and purpose and not allow us to shift from what God has called us to do.

For which cause we faint not; but though our outward man perish, yet the inward man is renewed day by day. For our light affliction, which is but for a moment, worketh for us a far more exceeding and eternal weight of glory; while we look not at the things which are seen, but at the things which are not seen: for the things which are seen are temporal; but the things which are not seen are eternal.

—II Corinthians 4:16-18

Chapter 6

Bringing It Full Circle

We are definitely living in the last days of the church, Jesus said in Rev. 22:12, Behold, I come quickly; and my reward *is* with me, to give every man according as his work shall be. As we are aligning ourselves for what God designed and created us for, before the foundation of the world, we can't allow anything or anyone to make us shift our assignment. We want to make sure that we are aligned with God's Word so we can fulfill the plan and purpose we were created and designed for by God. We don't want to leave this earth and not complete our assignments and be found out of alignment with God our creator. The Bible says in St. John 4:34, Jesus saith unto them, my meat is to *do the* will of him that sent me, and to *finish* his *work*. St. John 17:4, I have glorified thee on *the* earth: I have finished *the work* which thou gavest me to *do*.

When we allow ourselves to stop dreaming, stop pushing, stop trusting, and stop pressing and believing, we diminish our existence and Gods plans to work in our lives. The Word of God is food to the soul and nourishment to the body, Jesus said in St. Matthew 4:4 (ESV) "It is written, Man shall not live by bread alone, but by every word that comes from the mouth of God. We also need the Spirit of God which gives us life just as we need oxygen or a breathing machine to keep us alive. The *Spirit of* God hath made me, and the *breath of* the Almighty hath given me *life*, Job 33:4.

In order for his vision, purpose and dreams to continue to grow in our lives we have to diligently apply Gods Word. Reading and studying our Bible daily, along with praying for understanding, we can watch how God will begin to change our lives for the better. This is simply a part of Gods process to develop grow and mature our lives for his glory. We must continue to have a thirst and hunger for God's plan for our lives because Jesus said in St. John 4:14 (ESV) "But whoever drinks of the water that I will give him will never be thirsty again. The water that I will give him will become in him a spring of water welling up to eternal life." Jesus was referring to being filled with his Holy Spirit that completely satisfies and fulfill our lives totally. Therefore let us draw near with a true heart in full assurance of faith, with our hearts sprinkled clean from an evil conscience and our bodies washed with pure water, Hebrews 10:22 (ESV)

Once we understand God's process, we can begin to start putting things into place. As we acknowledge him, we then establish why we really need him in our lives both spiritually and naturally. Then we can began to get into prayer daily, study his word, and then we can repent of any wrong doing so we can walk in obedience according to his will and his word for our lives.

Those who start and stop, really don't trust the process of where God is taking them. In the world today, people want everything right now; no one wants to wait, through God process of development so we can receive what he has promise us, therefore we need to learn how to be patience when God is processing us. When we allow patience in our life God process will work out for our good, In James 1:3-4, states knowing *this*, that the trying of your faith worketh patience. But let patience have her perfect work, that ye may be perfect and entire, wanting nothing. An example of God process working through time for us is like the mixing of concrete as a solid foundation to build upon, and if we don't allow the right amount of time for the concrete to dry and set the foundation want be sold in our lives, II Timothy 2:19 says, Nevertheless the foundation of God standeth sure, having this seal, The Lord knoweth them that are his. And, Let everyone that nameth the name of Christ depart from iniquity. Which means if we don't patiently wait to hear what God is saying to us but are always in a hurry, we will not allow our mind to process and develop during the waiting period, and we are going to mess up what God is planning to grow and develop within us. We must not always be in a rush; by being impatience, we must learn to sit, wait and trust what God is developing and doing in our lives. As we pray, study and obey Gods Word, our lives will begin to change for the better. The more we allow the Word of God to sink deep down in our souls, we are allowing his word to break up the old fallow ground and to remove our old foundation which will allow God to build his new foundation in us, Hosea 10:12&13 says, Sow to yourselves in righteousness, reap in mercy; break up your fallow ground: for *it is* time to seek the LORD, till he come and rain righteousness upon you. Ye have plowed wickedness, ye have reaped iniquity; ye have eaten the fruit of lies: because thou didst trust in thy way, in the multitude of thy mighty men. It's imperative that we study, pray and obey his word on a daily basis that our total and complete life will align in the same direction that we can achieve Gods purpose and plan for our lives. We must never allow our lives to relapse or lose focus and return back to our old life style. True alignment in one's life is when we are operating in God's plan, will and purpose which God designed for us. The Word of God will truly align our lives in complete harmony and total unity with Jesus Christ. We must *Trust*, *Believe*, and *Wait*; and Gods process will truly come to pass. We must allow ourselves to become rooted, grounded and settled in God's Word so we can fulfill his plan for our lives.

> *If ye continue in the faith grounded and settled, and be not moved away from the hope of the gospel, which ye have heard, and which was preached to every creature which is under heaven; whereof I Paul am made a minister.*
>
> —Colossians 1:23

> *As ye have therefore received Christ Jesus the Lord, so walk ye in him: Rooted and built up in him, and stablished in the faith, as ye have been taught, abounding therein with thanksgiving.*
>
> —Colossians 2:6-7

Chapter 7

The Glorious Outcome from Staying Rooted and Grounded

But thanks be to God, which giveth us the victory through our Lord Jesus Christ. Therefore, my beloved brethren, be ye stedfast, unmoveable, always abounding in the work of the Lord, forasmuch as ye know that your labour is not in vain in the Lord.

—1 Corinthians 15:57–58

As we look into life, and realize that we all need to be rooted and grounded in Christ. If we are not rooted and grounded in Christ, we will be like the waves on the sea tossed to-and-fro, not knowing what to do or which way to go in life. It's imperative that our life be stable in Christ Jesus and that we align ourselves with God's Word so that we may take hold of eternal life. Then the outcome of our life from this moment on depends on the decisions that we make. We can choose to be rooted and grounded in God's Word or we can choose to live disconnected from the Word of God. For the Lord knoweth the way of the righteous: but *the way of the ungodly shall perish*, Psalm 1:6.

We must also be patience and allow the roots of God's Word to sink deeply within us, and then we can watch his process develop us, because God's Word will surely come to pass. In Psalm 92:12–15 it says; The righteous shall flourish like the palm tree: he shall grow like a cedar in Lebanon. Those that be planted in the house of the Lord shall flourish in the courts of our God. They shall still bring forth fruit in old age; they shall be fat and flourishing; to shew that the Lord *is upright: he is my rock, and there is no unrighteousness in him.*

We must stay planted in the row (path) in which we have been assigned. When we step out of the row (path), we are being uprooting from permanently being rooted in the Word of God. Roots that are not stable are roots that are not deeply planted, and they are not permanently attached to the soil therefore, they produce no stability for consist growth.

The consistency of the roots that are planted in good soil and on good ground will not be shaken or up rooted in the time of adverse conditions. The life of a tree is found in its root; you may want to cut down the tree because you don't want it in your yard or near your home anymore, but if you don't remove the tree from the roots, it will eventually grow back again, because the life and growth of the tree is contained in its roots and the tree gets its nourishment and supply for growth through its roots as well. The Bible teaches us in Job 14:7–9, For there is hope of a tree, If it be cut down, that it will sprout again, And that the tender branch thereof will not cease. Though the root thereof wax old in the earth, and the stock thereof die in the ground;

Yet through the scent of water it will bud, and bring forth branches like a plant. When our lives are rooted and grounded in God's Word, the enemy (Satan) cannot stop what God has planted and is developing in our lives.

God is our source, and he is looking for someone he can impart his will and plan into; he is looking for the right soil, to plant his purpose (as a seed) to accomplish his plan in the earth. Every seed that is planted by God will need rain and moisture for it to grow to its full potential and complete mature development. The true principle of God planting the seed of his Word in our lives will surely come to pass in the right season in our lives. Our hearts were created by God to carry out his will and to bring forth the fruit of righteousness when his Word is properly and permanently planted in our lives. Just as a seed has to remain in the ground over time to germinate, so the Word of God has to abide in us and in the right season of time, it will produce a glorious and fruitful outcome in our lives. Jesus said it best in St. John 15:7, if ye abide in me, and my words abide in you ye shall ask what ye will, and it shall be done unto you. In others words, God will pour out his blessing on all those who work the principles of his Word, because God is not a man that can lie. In Numbers 23:19 it is recorded, *God is not a man that* he should *lie*; neither the son of man that he should repent: hath he said, and shall he *not do it? or hath he spoken, and shall he not make it good?* God wants to live in us, and he wants his Word to be made *alive* in us. Therefore, our life has to be cultivated through the quickening of his Word and irrigated through the rain of his Spirit.

When planting seeds in the ground of our heart, we have to be sure that they are planted deep enough, so when the winds, storms, and floods of adversity of life come, they won't move us away from our stable position and location, but we will remain rooted and stable throughout every seasons in life. The Bible teaches us in II Corinthians 4:8–9, We are troubled on every side, yet not distressed; we are perplexed, but not in despair; Persecuted, but not forsaken; cast down, but not destroyed. We must also make sure that God's Word is planted so deep into the soil of are heart that when the sun comes up, it won't burn up the seed, to be scorched and die. In other words, if our life is deep enough in God Word, we won't be persuaded by people or other things that are designed by Satan to pluck us up from being planted in God's Word. Our lives through obedience is founded and grounded in Jesus Christ who is the solid rock. We find the example of this in Psalm 18:2 (NIV), The LORD *is* my rock, and my fortress, and my deliverer; My God, my rock, in whom I take refuge. He is my shield and the horn of my salvation, my stronghold. Also in St. Matthew 7:24-27 Therefore whosoever heareth these sayings of mine, and doeth them, I will liken him unto a wise man, which built his house upon a rock: and the rain descended, and the floods came, and the winds blew, and beat upon that house; and it fell not: for it was founded upon a rock. And every one that heareth these sayings of mine, and doeth them not, shall be likened unto a foolish man, which built his house upon the sand: and the rain descended, and the floods came, and the winds blew, and beat upon that house; and it fell: and great was the fall of it.

Every seed that is planted by God must be tested through time to allow it to produce in our lives. We as God's people will be tested to grow, developed and to produce the fruitfulness that he requires in our lives. When we are planted by God as his seed, he will make it grow up fully into complete maturity in his own time. Paul said in Philippians 1:6 (TPT), I pray with great faith for you, because I'm fully convinced that the One who began this gracious work in you will faithfully continue the process of maturing you until the unveiling of our Lord Jesus Christ. We must continue to grow through the test of time so that we can become what God created us to be. We must also be planted deep enough in God's Word so that when the tempter (Satan) comes, we will not be moved away from our establish place in God Word. We won't be persuaded or influenced to move to the left or the right but will stay planted and focus so the blessings of the Lord will continue to flow in our lives and we will accomplish what he created us for, in this process called life. The Bible teaches us in St. John 15:5, I am the vine, ye are the branches: He that abideth in me, and I in him, the same bringeth forth much fruit: for without me ye can do nothing.

When we stay where God plants us and allow his roots to settle permanently within us, God will grow and mature us and make us his own. In St. John 10:27–30, My sheep hear my voice, and I know them, and they follow me: and I give unto them eternal life; and they shall never perish, neither shall any *man* pluck them out of my hand. My Father, which gave *them* me, is greater than all; and no *man* is able to pluck *them* out of my Father's hand. I and my Father are one. In Jeremiah 24:6 the Lord declares unto us, For I will set mine eyes upon them for good, and I will bring them again to this land: and I will build them, and not pull *them* down; and I will plant them, and not pluck *them* up.

This is why it's so imperative to stay connected to the Word and will of God because negative things will always try to attach themselves to us and pull us away from being rooted and grounded in God.

We must never allow the opinions of others to make us change our mind of who we were designed to be in Christ. We must always remember that Satan is the enemy to our growth and full development, for the Bible declares in St. John 10:10 that Satan comes for three reasons: (1) to steal, (2) to kill, and (3) to destroy. Then he always tries to bring confusion before God can get us to see the benefits of obeying his Word. Satan doesn't want us to see the Word of God for what it truly is and what it truly does, and his job is to keep us away from God and out of alignment with God and his Word. He tries to place fear and doubt in the hearts and minds of God's people, and cause us not to seek to know the true and living God for ourselves. Jesus said in his Word, the Holy Spirit's job is to open our minds and hearts to the plan and purposes of God. God's Word is a Light in a dark world. St. Luke 4:18 Jesus stated that; The Spirit of the Lord *is* upon me, Because he hath anointed me to preach the gospel to the poor; He hath sent me to heal the brokenhearted, to preach deliverance to the captives, and recovering of sight to the blind, to set at liberty them that are bruised, to preach the acceptable year of the Lord. Once our eyes have been opened, we will clearly see the plan, the purpose, and the power of God being demonstrated in our life.

This reminds me of the Word of God that teaches us about the parable of a sower. When we really look back over the patterns of our lives through the Word of God, we will see ourselves inside the parables of God. Parables are earthly stories, but they have a heavenly meaning and when we work the total principles of his Word we will have a glorious outcome for our lives. The bible teaches us in St. Mark 4:2-9; And he taught them many things by parables, and said unto them in his doctrine, Hearken; Behold, there went out a sower to sow: and it came to pass, as he sowed, some fell by the way side, and the fowls of the air came and devoured it up. And some fell on stony ground, where it had not much earth; and immediately it sprang up, because it had no depth of earth: but when the sun was up, it was scorched; and because it had no root, it withered away. And some fell among thorns, and the thorns grew up, and choked it, and it yielded no fruit. And other fell on good ground, and did yield fruit that sprang up and increased; and brought forth, some thirtyfold, and some sixtyfold, and some an hundredfold. And he said unto them, He that hath ears to hear, let him hear what the spirit is saying to the church. In understanding this parable and the conditions of the soil (our heart) under which the seeds fell determined whether they grew and how lasting and fruitful their growth would become. As we feed our faith and starve our doubts through prayer, studying, and obeying God's Word and seeking Him in earnestly, our hearts and lives will overflow with the abundance of God's grace and spring forth as a great harvest of increase.

As I conclude this chapter I want you to envision the different types of grounds (conditions of one's heart) that Jesus desires to use for his purpose in the lives of his people. As Jesus described what the parable of the Sower means here in St. Mark 4:2-9, he's showing us the conditions of our heart towards God and how we receive his Word. The seed is the Word of God that is being sown to show us his plans and purposes for our lives. The wayside ground is when they have heard God's Word but never absorbed it and Satan came and immediately take it away, therefore it's no chance for growth. The stony ground is those who heard and received the Word with gladness and enthusiasm; however, they have no roots within themselves and when affliction or persecution arises for the word's sake, immediately they are offended and fall away. Those that were sown among thorns is like one who hears the Word, and the cares of this world, and the deceitfulness of riches, and the lusts of other things entering into their hearts, chokes the word, and it becomes unfruitful in their lives. Finally, in St. Mark 4:20 Jesus explains the seed sown on good ground, And these are they which are sown on good ground; such as hear the word, and receive *it*, and bring forth fruit. As a second reference in St. Luke 8:15, the good ground are they, which in an honest and good heart, having heard the word, keep *it*, and bring forth fruit with patience. The good ground are those who are seeking Jesus with their whole heart, mind and soul. They are the ones who hears, understands, receives and then applies God's Word to their lives. This allows God to accomplish his purpose and plans for our lives. May our faith and our lives exemplify the "good ground" (the good and honest heart) as recorded in God's Word. There can be no good outcome or glorious harvest for us if we don't have the good heart that Jesus explains to us in scripture. Remember it is the good ground that produces an abundant over flow of blessings and increase multiplied harvest in our lives. We are his creation; we are his workmanship and are handpicked, created, and designed by God himself, which God hath before ordained that we should walk in them, Ephesians 2:10.

When we align our lives with God's Word through prayer (acknowledging him), studying (establishing a relationship), repentance (spiritual cleansing) and obedience (trusting the process), God allows our lives to grow in such a way we will began to reap a harvest in him and have a glorious outcome, and our lives will began to produce and flourish with much fruit for the glory of God. In St. Mark 4:8, and St. Luke 8:15, it gives us a clear vision of the glorious outcome that we can look forward to. When the seed of God's Word fell on the good ground (our hearts), and it did yield fruit that sprang up and increased; and brought forth, some thirty, and some sixty, and some an hundredfold. Keeping God's Word in our hearts and going through the process and aligning ourselves with him comes down to this glorious outcome, "Faithfulness and Fruitfulness". As we think about how fruitful our life has been and how fruitful we want the remainder of our lives to be; we must continually pray that God will give us insight into his Word and the desire to be as fruitful as he has designed for us to be in him. Remember God's choicest and richest blessings are clearly contingent upon our obedience and devotion to following his laws and commandments for our lives. Finally the Bible says, our job and responsibility is to Fear God and to keep his commandments, for this *is* the whole *duty* of man. Ecclesiastes 12:13.

> *The blessing of the LORD, it maketh rich,*
> *And he addeth no sorrow with it.*
>
> —Proverbs 10:22

> *And let us not be weary in well doing: for in*
> *due season we shall reap, if we faint not.*
>
> —Galatians 6:9

> Hope *deferred maketh the heart sick: but when*
> *the desire cometh, it is* a tree of *life.*
>
> —Proverbs 13:12

> *O sing unto the LORD a new song; For he hath*
> *done marvellous things: His right hand, and his*
> *holy arm, Hath gotten him the* victory.
>
> —Psalm 98:1

> *It is better to trust in the Lord than to put confidence in man.*
>
> —Psalm 118:8

Rejoice in the Lord always: and again I say, Rejoice.

—Philippians 4:4

Thy seed will I establish forever, and build up thy throne to all generations. Selah.

—Psalm 89:4

Thine, O Lord is the greatness, and the power, and the glory, and the victory, and the majesty: for all that is in the heaven and in the earth is thine; thine is the kingdom, O Lord, and thou art exalted as head above all.

—I Chronicles 29:11

Rejoice evermore. Pray without ceasing. In everything give thanks: for this is the will of God in Christ Jesus concerning you.

—I Thessalonians 5:16-18

About the Author

Evangelist Demetra Billy, God's servant, was born and raised in Detroit, Michigan. The call to serve the Lord and walk out the plan and will for her life came at the age of fifteen. Since the time of her yes, God placed her in various positions of ministry in the body of Christ as a Junior Missionary to Missionary, overseeing the Youth Ministry, Mime Ministry, and Media Ministry, just to name a few. In January 2001, she answered the call to Evangelist and has dedicated her life even more to prayer, fasting, teaching, and preaching the Word of God. She has also devoted herself to staying aligned with God's Word by allowing the Lord to totally orchestrate her life. She is a licensed and ordained Evangelist alongside with her husband, Elder Wayne J. Billy Sr., where they are both Associate Ministers of Jesus Tabernacle of Deliverance Ministries in Detroit, Michigan. They are humbled and honored to serve under the pastorate of Apostle David and Pastor R. Elaine Billy. God has faithfully opened doors and made room for her gifts in the body of Christ. Although she has not birthed any natural children of her own, God has blessed her with seven children, fourteen grandchildren, seven godsons, and one goddaughter. God has placed a call and mandate upon her life to birth forth sons in the spirit into His kingdom. To God be the glory for the things he has done and for what is to come in the future.